Original title:
Mirrors of Reflection

Author: Olivia Orav
ISBN HARDBACK: 978-1-80560-964-3
ISBN PAPERBACK: 978-1-80561-525-5

Whispers of Autumn

Leaves crisp and golden, they dance with the breeze,
A tapestry woven, a sight that will please.
The sun dips low, casting hues of deep red,
While tales of the season linger unsaid.

The chill in the air, a soft sigh of change,
Nature's own palette, beautifully strange.
Squirrels gather acorns, their treasure to store,
Preparing for winter, they scurry and explore.

Fog rises gently, like whispers at dawn,
The world wrapped in silence, as daylight is drawn.
Each branch holds a secret, each shadow a song,
In this fleeting moment, feel where you belong.

Pumpkins ablaze, in fields they do glow,
As twilight descends, and the night starts to slow.
A crackling fire, with friends gathered near,
We share all our stories, laughter and cheer.

So cherish the magic that autumn bestows,
In every soft breeze, in each petal that blows.
For seasons may shift, but the beauty remains,
In whispers of autumn, our hearts find their chains.

Shifting Perspectives

In the mirror, shadows play,
Whispering truths in their own way.
What I see, may not be true,
Each angle shifts, reveals anew.

The world is wide, yet small, it seems,
Layers unfold like fragile dreams.
What was near, now feels afar,
Perspective changes who we are.

Wise Silhouettes

Beneath the trees, the shadows speak,
Echoes of wisdom for those who seek.
Steady forms against the sky,
In stillness, they teach us why.

With every dusk, they stretch and bend,
Telling tales that never end.
Silent watchers of the night,
Guiding us with their soft light.

The Nature of Clarity

Morning dew on blades of grass,
A moment caught, then fades to pass.
In stillness, thoughts begin to clear,
Truth appears when we draw near.

Beneath the noise, the heart will feel,
Every whisper, every reel.
Nature's touch brings gentle grace,
Illuminating every space.

Within the Frame

Pictures hang upon the wall,
Each one tells a story small.
Captured moments, frozen time,
Lives entwined in subtle rhyme.

Colors blend, then fade away,
Yet memories refuse to stay.
In every frame, a world confined,
Yet in our hearts, it's intertwined.

Gaze into the Abyss

In the depths where silence dwells,
A whisper calls, it binds, it spells.
The void, a mirror of the soul,
Lost thoughts in shadows, take their toll.

Time stands still, the heart will race,
Facing fears we can't erase.
In darkness, light begins to fade,
Yet within the dark, new paths are laid.

Shadows of Truth

Beneath the veil of twilight's gleam,
Whispers dance, a twisted dream.
Secrets linger in the air,
The truth unfolds with quiet flair.

In echoes soft, we find our way,
Through tangled lies that always sway.
Shadows stretch, contort and weave,
Yet in their depths, we dare believe.

The Duality of Me

In mirrored glass, reflections show,
Two sides of one, the bright, the low.
A battle fought, both light and dark,
In whispered thoughts, ignite the spark.

With every choice, a path unfolds,
Yet which is truth? The brave or bold?
I wear a mask, but underneath,
Lies a heart that seeks its sheath.

Beneath the Surface

Ripples dance on a tranquil sea,
Beneath, the chaos yearns to flee.
Secrets buried float and churn,
Lessons hidden, souls to learn.

In every wave, a story flows,
Unseen depths where wildness grows.
To dive below is to embrace,
The hidden truths in endless space.

Glassy Realms

Through visions clear, the waters gleam,
Reflections dance, like fleeting dreams.
In silence deep, the stillness sings,
A world untouched, where magic clings.

Dew-kissed petals in morning's light,
Sparkle soft, a pure delight.
Each ripple tells a tale of grace,
In glassy realms, we find our place.

Unveiled Realities

Shadows bend, the truth revealed,
In layers fine, our fates are sealed.
With every gaze, new worlds arise,
Unveiling dreams beneath the skies.

What once was lost, now comes to view,
In vibrant hues and shades so true.
Eclipsed by doubt, the light breaks free,
Unveiled realities call to me.

Whispers of the Past

In twilight's hush, the echoes play,
Softly weaving night and day.
Stories linger in the breeze,
Whispers of the past with ease.

Footsteps trace on ancient stone,
Memories linger, not alone.
In dreams we meet, in silence cast,
The tender tales from ages vast.

Fissures in the Light

When brightness breaks, new paths unfold,
In shadows deep, the truth is told.
A fragile thread, a gleaming spark,
Fissures in the light, not dark.

Yet through the cracks, we find our way,
Emerging strong, come what may.
In radiant shards, the colors blend,
Fissures in the light, our friend.

Mysteries in the Reflection

In shadows cast on still water,
Whispers dance beneath the surface.
Faces lost in fleeting moments,
Time unwinds its silent purpose.

Fragments of a hidden story,
Glimmer faintly in the light.
Every glance a fleeting echo,
Secrets veiled, yet ever bright.

Ripples carry thoughts unspoken,
Dreams adrift on silver streams.
What we see is not the whole,
Life is woven from our dreams.

As we peer into our depths,
Questions linger in the air.
What do we find in our gaze?
Expectations meet despair.

Every glance reflects a puzzle,
Pieces scattered, seeking form.
The heart knows a truth so subtle,
In the stillness, we transform.

The Echoing Soul

In the silence where we wander,
Voices trace the paths of thought.
Echoes linger, soft yet strong,
Resonating all we've sought.

Whispers of a thousand moments,
Carried forth on breaths of time.
Every sigh a tender story,
Every heartbeat like a rhyme.

Thoughts like shadows dance around,
In the corners of our mind.
What is felt is often deeper,
Than the words we leave behind.

In reflections, we hear the music,
Melodies of joy and pain.
Every note a fleeting memory,
In the chorus, we remain.

So we listen to the echoes,
Find the truth in every sound.
In this symphony of being,
All our hopes and fears are found.

Palettes of Perception

Colors swirl in vibrant strokes,
Life unveils its layered hues.
What we see is but a canvas,
Worn by shades of varied views.

Truth and doubt entwine like brushstrokes,
Mixing in the mind's great art.
Every glance is subjective,
Crafting worlds that set apart.

Rather than black or white choices,
Life presents a spectrum wide.
Waves of feelings, thoughts and choices,
In the palette where we bide.

As we blend our vivid moments,
Creating portraits of our fate,
Brush in hand, we paint our stories,
Transcending time, we navigate.

In the end, it's our creation,
What we hold transforms the soul.
Through the shades, our lives unfold,
In this masterpiece, we're whole.

Illusions Unbound

Beyond the veil of earthly vision,
Lies a world both vast and strange.
Boundaries blur in shifting light,
Fate and fortune rearrange.

Mirrors break and show us facets,
Of a self we hardly know.
What is real, and what is dream?
In the blend, we ebb and flow.

Underneath the surface glimmers,
Truths we've buried in the night.
As we seek the inner meaning,
Illusions fade, revealing light.

Choices made in fleeting moments,
Guide our steps along the way.
In the dance of life, each heartbeat,
Creates the dreams of yesterday.

So we walk with eyes wide open,
Finding magic in the mundane.
In the shadows, whispers beckon,
Illusions lost, the soul unchained.

Echoes of Unseen Truths

In shadows where silence dwells,
Whispers carry untold tales,
Lost among the fleeting cells,
Truths emerge as daylight pales.

Hidden realms of thought collide,
Secrets woven in the night,
Hearts embrace what minds deride,
Unraveled hopes take silent flight.

Footprints fade on winding trails,
Memories dance in soft embrace,
Beneath the weight of ancient pales,
Lies the essence of our grace.

Questions linger in the air,
Fingers trace the unseen lines,
Echoes rise from depths of care,
Searching for the light that shines.

In the void, a spark ignites,
Illuminating paths once lost,
Breaking through the endless nights,
Finding truth amidst the frost.

Shimmering Facades

Beneath a cloak of bright deceit,
Lies a world so far removed,
Polished smiles, a rare retreat,
In mirrored walls, truth is grooved.

Glisten softly in the light,
Attraction draws the weary gaze,
Flickering in day and night,
Such charm can mask the endless haze.

Langorous moments drift away,
With every dream, the colors fade,
Unraveling the grand display,
As fleeting joys slowly invade.

Yet, in whispers, echoes call,
Revealing depth within the gloss,
Faces change, yet shadows fall,
In the mirage, we count the loss.

With each layer, secrets fold,
Beneath the shine, the depth is bare,
Truth, a treasure often sold,
In facades spun with tender care.

Glassy Veil of Self

A sheen of glass, a fragile form,
Reflects the heart's concealed embrace,
In moments lost, beneath the storm,
Shadows dance with artful grace.

The edges blur, a wistful sigh,
Mapping thoughts of dreams unfurled,
Life's stories told with every cry,
Unseen glimpses of another world.

Fractured light, a haunting sight,
In the shatter lies the truth,
Refracting pain, hope takes flight,
Through the cracks, we find our youth.

Silence rings within the glass,
A wall constructed from our fears,
The deeper we dive, the more we pass,
To reveal what time endears.

Yet, within this veil, we see,
Quiet strength in shattered sheen,
For through the cracks, we can be free,
And build anew from what has been.

Reflections in Still Waters

Beneath the calm, a world awakes,
Rippling visions, soft and clear,
Every thought, the surface shakes,
Revealing depths we often fear.

Leaves float gently, time stands still,
In mirrored pools, we find our way,
A dance of light, a tranquil thrill,
As dreams and shadows lightly sway.

In every ripple, stories blend,
Silent echoes of who we are,
Distant journeys, paths we wend,
In reflected light, we find a star.

Yet stillness holds an aching truth,
Beneath the beauty lies the pain,
For every dawn that brings the youth,
Also carries whispers of the rain.

So gaze upon the waters deep,
And learn the art of letting flow,
In every reflection, secrets keep,
The heart's true essence starts to grow.

Hidden Depths

Beneath the surface, secrets lie,
Whispers of old, the softest sigh.
In shadows deep, the stories blend,
A journey where the heart must bend.

The depths conceal what eyes can't see,
In silent corners, we roam free.
With every breath, the layers peel,
What once was hidden, now reveals.

In pools of thought, reflections dance,
A fleeting moment, a second chance.
The tides will ebb, the winds will blow,
Yet hidden depths will always show.

Through tangled roots and veils of night,
We search for truth, we chase the light.
Each wave that crashes, each storm that stirs,
Unfolds the magic that always purrs.

So dive with courage, lose your fears,
Embrace the depth, the ocean of tears.
For in the darkest, deepest part,
Lies the reflection of the heart.

Reflections of the Heart

In stillness lies a gentle stream,
Mirrored moments, a silent dream.
Echoes of laughter, whispers of love,
Reflections dance like stars above.

Each ripple speaks of what once was,
A tender touch, a fleeting cause.
In crystal waters, our souls unfold,
With every glance, a story told.

As shadows stretch and daylight fades,
In twilight's grasp, the heart parades.
The softest echoes of what we feel,
In mirrored depths, our truths reveal.

In the quiet hush of fading light,
We gather hopes, embrace the night.
Each reflection shines with lessons learned,
A sacred fire that ever burns.

So let your heart be your guiding star,
In reflections, we find who we are.
The journey flows like rivers run,
In every heartbeat, we are one.

The Whispering Glass

In the dark night, a glass appears,
Whispers of truths, echoes of fears.
It shows the world through shades of gray,
A fragile touch, a silent play.

With breath held tight, we look within,
To face the light, to shed our skin.
Each reflection tells of love and pain,
A whispered secret, a soft refrain.

The glass reveals what we conceal,
The hidden dreams, the wounds that heal.
With every glance, the heart takes flight,
The shadows dance in the pale moonlight.

In gentle curves, our visions weave,
A tapestry of what we believe.
The whispering glass, a guiding light,
Leads through the darkness, into the bright.

So take a chance, embrace the grace,
Let whispers speak in this sacred space.
For in the glass, our stories twine,
A window to the soul divine.

Glimpses of What Lies Beneath

Beneath the calm, the storm does brew,
A hidden world, a vibrant hue.
In silent depths, the secrets flow,
Glimpses of what we yearn to know.

The surface shimmers, but there's more,
In shadows deep, a mystic lore.
With every pulse, the currents shift,
Unseen wonders, the heart's own gift.

In fleeting moments, we catch a glance,
A dance of echoes, a sacred chance.
The heart reveals what the mind might doubt,
In quiet whispers, we seek about.

As water churns and winds will wail,
We clutch the truth, we set our sail.
Glimpses of dreams that shimmer bright,
Guide us softly through the night.

So dive and plunge into the unknown,
Embrace the depths where love has grown.
For in each wave, a lesson lies,
Glimpses of truth beneath the skies.

Moments Captured in Daylight

Morning dew on blades of grass,
Sunlight dances, moments pass.
Laughter echoes, children play,
Joyful hearts embraced the day.

Amber rays through leaves filter,
Time stands still as pulses quiver.
Nature whispers, secrets shared,
In this light, we feel prepared.

Flowers bloom, their fragrance wide,
Butterflies all in their glide.
Every second wrapped in gold,
Fleeting tales of life unfold.

Evening comes, the shadows grow,
Softly, gently, breezes blow.
Memories linger, warm and bright,
Captured moments in the light.

As the sun dips low to sleep,
Promises of dreams we keep.
In this daylight, hopes arise,
Forever held beneath the skies.

A Glimpse Beyond

In the stillness of the night,
Stars above, they burn so bright.
Whispers float on silver streams,
Carried softly, woven dreams.

Time is but a fleeting glance,
Each heartbeat, a sacred chance.
Close your eyes and breathe it in,
Find the strength that lies within.

Mountains rise beyond our view,
Veils of mist, a different hue.
Every shadow hides a light,
Truths that shimmer in the night.

Journey forth, let spirits soar,
Seek the paths not walked before.
Every doubt will fade away,
With the dawn, there comes the day.

In the echoes of the past,
Lessons learned, so deep and vast.
A glimpse beyond the known expanse,
Life's a story, always dance.

The Dance of Shadows

Underneath the silver moon,
Shadows flicker, softly croon.
Figures sway on pavement worn,
Casts of night, the dance is born.

Whispers of the darkened trees,
Echo through the gentle breeze.
Every shape tells tales untold,
In the night, the bold, the bold.

Footsteps soft as whispered sighs,
Notes of melancholy rise.
As the stars begin to gleam,
In this rhythm, we find dream.

Every shadow has a tale,
Captured moments, they unveil.
In the dance, we lose our fears,
With each sway, the heart draws near.

Beneath the stars, we intertwine,
Fading into space and time.
In the twilight, stories flow,
In the dance of shadows, glow.

Riddles in the Glass

Through the window, worlds collide,
Reflections dance, they turn and glide.
Figures caught in endless spin,
Riddles whisper from within.

Every glimmer holds a clue,
Secrets shared, both old and new.
Fractured light on surfaces play,
Patterns shift and fade away.

Within the glass, a moment trapped,
Times we loved, and hearts unclapped.
As eyes wander, stories bloom,
In the light, dispel the gloom.

Fragments speak of lives once led,
Echoes of the words unsaid.
Gaze within; the magic's there,
Hidden truths in glass laid bare.

So take a moment, pause, and stare,
In these riddles, seek and dare.
Find the layers, deep and vast,
In the glass, our futures cast.

Echoes of the Self

In quiet moments, whispers breathe,
Old memories drift like autumn leaves.
Fragments of laughter linger still,
Mirrors crack, but hearts can heal.

Paths I wander, shadows wane,
Footsteps echo, life in vain.
Yet through the doubt, a flame ignites,
Guiding me through endless nights.

Each tear a story, each smile a song,
Carving a journey where we belong.
In the solitude, we find our might,
Embracing darkness to seek the light.

Layers peeling, truth revealed,
A tapestry of wounds unsealed.
Finding strength in what we hide,
In the echoes, we confide.

So let the whispers forge the way,
Into tomorrow, come what may.
For in the depths, a spark will gleam,
Awakening the silent dream.

In the Luminous Void

In the vastness where shadows play,
A silent pulse ignites the gray.
Stars whisper secrets, far and near,
Illuminating what we fear.

A dance of silence, void of sound,
In the emptiness, hope is found.
Soft glimmers birth a cosmic thread,
Where thoughts and wishes dare to tread.

The light reveals what's often masked,
In tranquil calm, we're unasked.
Facing depths, we shed our guise,
In the void, we touch the skies.

With every breath, we draw anew,
The endless night, a canvas blue.
Embrace the stillness, the unknown,
In the luminous, we are not alone.

For in the dark, we learn to soar,
Finding strength in evermore.
Each flicker speaks of dreams untold,
In the luminous, we find our gold.

Soft Reflections of Resolve

In tranquil water, ripples dance,
Mirrored dreams in quiet chance.
Soft reflections, thoughts arise,
Carving paths through open skies.

Roots of courage, deeply sown,
Through storms of doubt, we've bravely grown.
Each wave a lesson, flows to shore,
In gentle strength, we seek for more.

Moments linger, a tender grace,
Finding solace in this space.
Reflecting wishes, hopes in flight,
In every shadow, shines a light.

The heartbeats echo, steady and true,
In quiet resolve, we'll break through.
Gathering wisdom from every fall,
Soft reflections beckon us all.

Together weaving dreams so bright,
Through every trial, seek the light.
For in the calm, we find our voice,
Soft reflections, we rejoice.

The Play of Light and Shadow

In the theater of dusk and dawn,
Light and shadow dance upon the lawn.
Fleeting moments, colors collide,
In this play, our hopes reside.

Draped in silence, a story unfolds,
Whispers of passion, secrets told.
Veils of twilight, gently unfurl,
An intimate embrace with the world.

Every flicker, a heartbeat shared,
In the balance, we've dared.
Holding close to dreams that gleam,
In light's embrace, we find our theme.

With each transition, fear and grace,
In shadows, we learn to embrace.
For in the dark, we find our way,
The cadence of night, guiding day.

Together they weave, a tale divine,
In the tapestry, we intertwine.
For life's a stage with each new role,
In the play of light, we find the whole.

Layers of Being

Beneath the skin we wear,
A tapestry of thought,
Each thread a story shared,
In silence, battles fought.

The heart speaks in whispers,
Echoes of dreams untold,
Like petals in the wind,
Soft yet fiercely bold.

We're shadows in daylight,
And light within the dark,
Masked by our own fears,
Yet glowing with a spark.

Each layer has its color,
A spectrum we explore,
With courage as our guide,
Unlocking every door.

In the depth of our being,
We find our truest song,
Interwoven with the world,
Where all souls belong.

The Stillness Speaks

In quietude, I find,
A rhythm soft and deep,
Where thoughts like rivers flow,
And secrets choose to keep.

The morning light awakens,
With whispers on the breeze,
A song of tranquil moments,
That dances through the trees.

With each breath, a story,
The silence paints a scene,
A canvas broad and timeless,
Where peace can intervene.

In stillness, eyes are opened,
To vistas yet unseen,
A journey based on feeling,
Where heart and mind convene.

As shadows gently linger,
And twilight starts to creep,
The world, in hushed surrender,
Finds solace in its sleep.

Silhouette and Light

A figure stands in twilight,
Outlined against the sky,
Where shadows kiss the sun,
As day begins to die.

With every bend and angle,
A story starts to weave,
In whispers of the evening,
A tale that all believe.

The dance of dark and bright,
A balance pure and true,
In every breath, a moment,
Of red, of gold, of blue.

In silhouette, we wander,
Through paths both old and new,
Embracing every contour,
In lines that stir the view.

For life is but a canvas,
Where shadows play their part,
In every line and shadow,
We find the beating heart.

Traces of the Unseen

In the quiet, they linger,
Footprints on the soul,
Invisible connections,
That weave and bind us whole.

A glance, a passing smile,
Threads of what's felt but small,
In echoes of existence,
Resonating through it all.

The memories paint our canvas,
In hues of soft regret,
Yet hope is always whispering,
A promise, with no debt.

In every heartbeat, shadows,
Mark the path we tread,
Traces of the unseen,
In words we've never said.

A tapestry of moments,
Woven fine and tight,
In the depth of our being,
We find the purest light.

Reflections of Time

In the mirror of the past,
Dreams flicker like a flame.
Whispers from long ago,
Echoes still bear our name.

Seasons change with silent grace,
Leaves fall, a soft goodbye.
Moments linger, fade away,
Yet in memory, they lie.

Time is a gentle thief,
Stealing the hours we hold.
Yet through our hearts it weaves,
Stories of silver and gold.

The clock ticks with muted sound,
Drawing lines on our face.
Each wrinkle tells a tale,
Of love, loss, and embrace.

Looking back with tender eyes,
We gather the scattered years.
Reflections lead us forward,
Through laughter and through tears.

Fractured Visions

Shards of dreams scatter wide,
Glints of light in the dark.
Reality bends and sways,
Each thought leaves a mark.

Colors bleed, collide, and blend,
Truth hides behind the veil.
Fragments of distorted hope,
In shadows, we exhale.

Perception warps and twists,
Fleeting glimpses of the whole.
Through the cracks, we build anew,
Searching deep for the soul.

Vision blurred, yet we strive,
To piece what we can find.
In the chaos, beauty blooms,
Within the fractured mind.

Holding tight to the pieces,
In this dance of disarray,
From the ruins, we arise,
Creating light from gray.

Luminous Introspection

In the stillness of the night,
Thoughts like stars begin to glow.
Dancing gently on the edge,
Of all that we might know.

A soft radiance in our minds,
Illuminates the way.
Each question, a flicker bright,
In the shadows where we play.

Clarity emerges slow,
In a world of restless dreams.
Through reflection's tender gaze,
Truth reveals its silver seams.

The heart knows its secret song,
A melody full of grace.
Luminous paths guide us forth,
In this sacred, tranquil space.

With every thought, a spark ignites,
Awakening the soul's delight.
Through introspection, we ascend,
Shining brightly, we take flight.

The Veil of Self

In layers thin, we hide away,
Wrapped in fears, our shadows play.
A curtain drawn, a faint disguise,
Waiting for the truth to rise.

Beneath the surface, whispers dwell,
Echoes of a silent spell.
Through the veil, we long to see,
The essence of what we could be.

Masks we wear in fleeting roles,
Concealing deep, unfathomed souls.
Yet beneath this fragile skin,
Lives the light we hold within.

To lift the veil, a brave endeavor,
Bringing heart and spirit together.
In vulnerability, strength is found,
The truest self can then astound.

With each step, we shed the past,
Embracing what will ever last.
The veil falls gently to the ground,
And in our truth, we are unbound.

Infinite Reflections

In the stillness of the night,
Mirrors hold the truth so bright.
Whispers dance on silver waves,
Echoes fill the silent caves.

Thoughts collide in a gentle stream,
Fragments of a fading dream.
Time unfolds in soft embrace,
Unraveling each hidden space.

Gazing deep in crystal pools,
Finding warmth in ancient rules.
Every glance a story told,
Boundless tales in hues of gold.

Catch the shimmer of the past,
Reflections flicker, shadows cast.
Infinite paths intertwine,
Life's reflections, yours and mine.

We are but a fleeting spark,
Dancing brightly in the dark.
Endless journeys, never cease,
In this mirror, find your peace.

When Light Meets Shadow

In the dance of day and night,
Where darkness fades, embracing light.
Shadows stretch, they whisper low,
A story told in ebb and flow.

Golden rays brush the ground,
Silhouettes in silence found.
Each heartbeat vivid, softly glows,
In the twilight, magic grows.

Gentle hues begin to blend,
Promises of hope descend.
As the sun begins to wane,
Night unveils its soft refrain.

Crescent moons and twinkling stars,
Twilight fades, the evening's ours.
Where light kisses shadow's cheek,
In their union, truth we seek.

Moments linger, soft and sweet,
Life's duality, we repeat.
In the balance, hearts align,
Finding solace, love enshrined.

The Soul's Reflection

In the mirror of the soul,
Glimmers of our essence whole.
Each glance reveals unseen grace,
Truth unfolds in time and space.

Mysteries swirl in every gaze,
Chasing dreams in endless maze.
Whispers echo, shadows speak,
Journey inward, strong not meek.

Layers soft like morning dew,
Unraveling the vibrant hue.
Each heartbeat a gentle guide,
Inward paths that coincide.

Sacred light in darkness found,
Reflections spiral all around.
Through the chaos, find the calm,
Healing balm, a soothing psalm.

We are threads in woven fate,
Every soul we touch, create.
In the depths, find love's embrace,
Reflection lost in time and space.

Faces in the Night

In the stillness, shadows creep,
Whispers hidden, secrets keep.
Every face a tale to weave,
In the darkness, we believe.

Glimmers caught in moonlight's sheen,
Flickering hints of what's unseen.
Eyes like lanterns, bright and keen,
In the night, a silent scene.

Footsteps echo, soft and slow,
Underneath the twilight's glow.
Each heartbeat resonates with fear,
Faces fade, yet stay so near.

Ghostly figures, intertwine,
Carrying dreams, yours and mine.
In the quiet, lost in thought,
Living moments time has wrought.

As the stars begin to wane,
Life's illusions, joy and pain.
In the dark, bonds intertwine,
Faces linger, yours in mine.

Silhouettes in the Twilight

Shadows dance on the edges of night,
Whispers echo in the fading light.
Figures stand tall against the sky,
Lost in dreams that drift and fly.

Stars flicker, ancient and bright,
Guiding hearts through the darkened blight.
Moonbeams waltz on the ground below,
Painting paths where the soft winds blow.

Time unravels in the dusk's embrace,
Every silhouette finds its grace.
The world tilts in this twilight hour,
Breathing life into forgotten power.

As shadows merge in a fleeting blend,
Moments captured, our souls transcend.
In the twilight, we find what's true,
Silhouettes whispering, me and you.

Fragmented Whispers of Identity

Mirrors reflect a shattered view,
Pieces of self in shades askew.
Each voice whispers a different tale,
Echoes of dreams that momentarily pale.

Masks worn thin in the morning light,
Searching for courage to stand and fight.
Identity splintered across the floor,
Fragments scattered, yearning for more.

Truth concealed behind many a guise,
In between laughter and fleeting sighs.
Chasing shadows of who we once were,
In the silence, our thoughts softly stir.

As we gather these pieces anew,
Building a vision that feels like you.
Identity's quilt, stitched with care,
A tapestry woven in the open air.

Whispers of self carry on the breeze,
Learning to be whole with gentle ease.
Finding strength in every blend,
Fragmented whispers, we shall mend.

The Surface that Lies Beneath

Ripples dance on waters clear,
A world hidden, drawing near.
Beneath the calm, stories swirl,
Unseen wonders that gently twirl.

Through the depths, shadows creep,
Secrets held in silence deep.
The surface smooth, a tranquil lie,
Veiling truths that none can shy.

Echoes of life, both silent and loud,
Bubbles rise from beneath the shroud.
Journey down where the currents flow,
Discover what the surface won't show.

In the stillness, thoughts collide,
A hidden realm where dreams abide.
Waves of insight crash and break,
The surface trembles, hearts awake.

Diving deep, unearthing the gray,
Finding light in the disarray.
For every layer that we unearth,
The deeper truth reveals its worth.

Lenses of Lost Moments

Life's a series of fleeting frames,
Captured glimpses, cherished names.
Through the lens, we seek and find,
Moments lost, yet intertwined.

Snapshots etched in memory's art,
Each a whisper from the heart.
Fleeting time, mirages strong,
Melodies of where we belong.

Reflections cast in a playful light,
Chasing shadows that feel so right.
Fragmented joy, stained with tears,
Through the lens, we confront our fears.

Every shutter click tells a tale,
Of love and loss, we set sail.
In the stillness, we pause and sigh,
Lenses of moments that never die.

As we watch the world unfurl,
Through our eyes, every swirl.
Echoes linger, memories rise,
Lost moments twinkling in our eyes.

The Broken Spectrum

Colors fade, yet still they blend,
A fractured light that won't pretend.
Hidden shades in quiet skies,
Whispers of truth in muted lies.

Shadows dance where dreams once soared,
In the silence, hope's restored.
A prism caught in time's cruel hand,
Fragments scattered on the land.

Every hue a tale to tell,
Moments lost, and some that fell.
A rainbow cuts through darkest night,
In brokenness, we find our light.

Spectrum wide yet held so close,
A journey crafted with each dose.
For in the cracks, new colors rise,
To paint the world beyond our eyes.

Unfolding Truths

Layers peel in quiet grace,
Revealing depths we often chase.
Truths embraced, yet hard to find,
Within the heart and in the mind.

Moments pass, like whispers blown,
In each breath, a seed is sown.
What we seek is buried deep,
In shadows where our fears do creep.

Unraveling tales the past has spun,
Threads of sorrow, threads of fun.
Light breaks through the fragile veil,
As we chart our inner trail.

With every step, more is revealed,
What once was lost, now is healed.
In the mirror where we stand,
The truths unfold, like grains of sand.

The Tapestry of Self

Woven threads of joy and pain,
Each distinct, yet never plain.
Colors blend, a vibrant scene,
In every moment, what has been.

Patterns form, then shift and sway,
Life's design in bright array.
Every stitch a choice defined,
Crafting tales of heart and mind.

Embroidered dreams and scars alike,
Each layer tells of love and strife.
Frayed edges tell of battles fought,
In this fabric, lessons taught.

Intricate knots in every fold,
Stories whispered, brave and bold.
In the loom of life, we find,
Unity in the entwined.

Beyond the Veil

Silhouettes drift in quiet night,
Dust of stars, a ghostly light.
What we see is but a part,
Of the wonders that touch the heart.

Veils of time obscure our view,
Yet the whispers call us through.
Mysteries wrapped in soft embrace,
In shadows, we seek for grace.

Glimpses flash from worlds unknown,
Each reflection, seeds are sown.
Eclipsing fears, we take the leap,
Into the depths where secrets keep.

Bridges built from dreams we share,
Transcending moments, we lay bare.
Beyond the veil, we learn to see,
The beauty of what's meant to be.

Portraits of the Heart

In the frame of quiet love,
Every glance a gentle touch,
Colors blend from hue to hue,
A canvas brushed with soft such.

Whispers painted on the walls,
Stories held in fleeting sighs,
Each heartbeat a brushstroke bold,
Capturing dreams beneath the skies.

In shadows deep where secrets hide,
A portrait speaks without a word,
Capturing the light inside,
In silence, feeling is stirred.

Faces come and faces go,
Yet the essence lingers near,
Every laugh a vivid glow,
Memories crafted, crystal clear.

Through the lens of tender trust,
We uncover each hidden flaw,
In these portraits, we find us,
A masterpiece without a law.

Surfaces and Depths

With each wave that brushes shore,
The ocean tells tales untold,
Beneath the surface, secrets roar,
Mysteries in the deep unfold.

Reflections glimmer in the sun,
Yet shadows linger far below,
What is seen is just a run,
Of what the heart may never show.

The calm belies the storms we hide,
Moments lost in restless seas,
Yet every current's gentle glide,
Whispers softly through the breeze.

In each tide, a lesson learned,
The balance of the loud and still,
From chaos, sweet understanding earned,
To navigate with grace and will.

Thus we dive, unafraid to sink,
To find the depths within our core,
In the waters, we pause to think,
That both surface and depth explore.

Collisions of Identity

In the clash of thoughts and dreams,
Voices blend, then split apart,
Each unique thread it seems,
Weaving the fabric of the heart.

Masks are worn in daylight's glow,
Layers thickened, peeling slow,
Beneath the guise, who do we know?
The truth dances in shadow's flow.

Connections spark with subtle grace,
In laughter shared, in tears shed,
In the chaos, we find our place,
Through the stories we've all read.

The puzzle pieces fit and break,
A mosaic shaped by love and pain,
From every collision, we awake,
Finding joy in the beautiful rain.

So let us collide with open hearts,
Embrace the fractures, stitch the rift,
In the beauty of these parts,
Our identities, a treasured gift.

The Quiet Refrain

In the stillness, echoes sigh,
Words unspoken softly drift,
A melody beneath the sky,
Carrying the heart's sweet gift.

The rhythm of a life well-lived,
Plays softly on an unseen stage,
With every note, the soul is sieved,
Turning pages, turning age.

In the pause, where time stands still,
A tune persists, though faint and small,
In silence, we begin to fill,
The spaces left when shadows call.

Through the quiet, truths arise,
Introspection paints the air,
In the heart, a gentle prize,
Refrains of love, both soft and rare.

Embrace the still, let music soar,
Feel the weight of every strain,
In the quiet, we explore,
A life's song, our sweet refrain.

Through Crystal Eyes

Through crystal eyes, the world we see,
A kaleidoscope of dreams set free.
Colors dance in soft, golden light,
Whispers of magic in the night.

In every glance, a story unfolds,
The secrets of life, gently told.
Mirrors reflect what the heart can't hide,
Journey within where shadows abide.

Glimmers of hope in a tear's gentle fall,
Through crystal eyes, we rise and we stall.
Nature's grace in each fleeting breath,
Capturing moments that dance with death.

The world spins on with a tender grace,
Every heartbeat a sacred place.
Through crystal eyes, all fears dissolve,
In this embrace, our souls evolve.

Counting Reflections

In the mirror, I count my thoughts,
Fragments of dreams, battles I fought.
Each reflection, a moment's grace,
Tracing the lines on my weathered face.

Echoes of laughter, shadows of pain,
Counting reflections like drops of rain.
Time flows slow, yet swiftly it flies,
In the stillness, the past never dies.

I gather my wisdom, piece by piece,
In each reflection, I find my peace.
Lessons learned under stormy skies,
Through every trial, my spirit will rise.

With every glance, new layers appear,
Unraveling truths, shedding my fear.
In counting reflections, I find my way,
Guided by stars that lead me each day.

Inward Journeys

Inward journeys, we delve so deep,
Through valleys of silence, where shadows creep.
Footprints of wisdom, we softly trace,
In the heart's quiet, we find our space.

Each turn reveals what the mind conceals,
The pulse of our being, the truth that heals.
Amidst the chaos, a whisper so clear,
Inward journeys draw us near.

Beneath the surface, treasures await,
We navigate love, fear, and fate.
Mapping the shadows, we learn to glide,
Inward journeys, a sacred ride.

Every sorrow a lesson, every joy a song,
In the depths of our hearts, we belong.
In stillness, we gather, we quietly yearn,
Inward journeys teach us to learn.

The Dimmed Luminance

In twilight's grip, the dimmed luminance,
Flickers gently, a lost romance.
Stars awaken with a wistful sigh,
Painting whispers across the sky.

Silhouettes dance in the fading glow,
Embers of dreams that we used to know.
Each breath a memory, soft and sweet,
The dimmed luminance beneath our feet.

Time softly tugs at the edges of light,
Carving shadows that fade from sight.
Yet in this darkness, hope finds its way,
Guiding the lost, igniting the day.

With every heartbeat, a flicker ignites,
In the dimmed luminance, we find our fights.
Emerging anew from shadows that bind,
The light of our souls, forever aligned.

Refractions of Forgotten Dreams

In twilight's embrace, shadows play,
Whispers of hopes drift away.
Memories flicker, dimly they gleam,
Lost in the tides of a silenced dream.

Dancing on edges of fragile time,
Echoes of laughter, a distant chime.
Captured in glass, reflections twist,
Fragments of moments that once coexisted.

Silken threads of color fade,
In the fabric of night, the colors cascade.
Fleeting visions, barely seen,
Carried on winds where dreams convene.

Beneath the surface, ripples sigh,
Unseen currents gently glide by.
Each shimmer carries a whispered theme,
Reflections of what could have been a dream.

In the depths of forgotten lore,
A tapestry woven, behind closed doors.
Lattice of wishes, in shadows they gleam,
Embraced in whispers of a fading dream.

A Tapestry of Doubts

Woven in silence, the threads intertwine,
Doubts like shadows unfurl and align.
In the corners where worries breed,
Fears find comfort, igniting the need.

Stitch by stitch, a fabric takes form,
Patterns of chaos, restless in storm.
Glimmers of hope, they flicker and fade,
A maze of decisions, the path often swayed.

In the loom of the night, questions arise,
Each thread a whisper, deceptive disguise.
Bound by the weight of all that we hold,
Tales of uncertainty, meticulously told.

Under the glow of impending forks,
Doubts congregate, like silent storks.
Carried in burdens, we wander alone,
In a world of choices not fully our own.

Yet in every thread, a story sleeps,
Awaiting the moment when courage leaps.
For in the tapestry, we find our way,
Connecting the doubts, come what may.

The Other Side of Clarity

Beneath the surface, clear as the sea,
Lies a pool of questions, both wild and free.
Obscured by layers, the truth intertwines,
In the heart of confusion, clarity shines.

Veils of perception shift and sway,
In the mirror of minds, reflections play.
Moments of stillness, where silence prevails,
Lead to the wisdom that often exhales.

Through the haze, light finds a way,
Illuminating paths where shadows lay.
Navigating currents both fierce and bold,
Unraveling stories, quietly told.

With each revelation, a distance shrinks,
The courage to see, the heart often thinks.
Embracing the uncertain, we dance in the light,
Finding solace in chaos, a beacon so bright.

The other side beckons, a shimmer, a gleam,
Where clarity blooms like a radiant dream.
In the depths of the mind, it fiercely ignites,
Guiding the lost to their destined heights.

Bubbles of Consciousness

Floating gently in the vast unknown,
Bubbles of thought, seeds of our own.
Each one a wonder, a fleeting flight,
A glimmer of wisdom, dancing in light.

Drifting through currents, fragile and bright,
Carrying whispers, shadows ignite.
In the silence, a voice softly hums,
Echoes of knowledge, softly it comes.

Bubbles collide, creating a storm,
A tapestry woven, each one a form.
Sharing the stories, the joys, the fears,
A harmony crafted through laughter and tears.

In the ebb and the flow, connections arise,
Reflecting the vastness of all in our eyes.
With each little pop, a lesson unfolds,
In the mystery of life, the universe holds.

So let us embrace these bubbles we see,
Navigating the vastness, forever set free.
For in every moment, there lies a chance,
To dance with our thoughts in this cosmic dance.

Lurking Beneath

In shadows deep, secrets hide,
Whispers echo, nowhere to confide.
Beneath the calm, waters churn,
Yearning for the flame's return.

Silent footsteps, a chilling breeze,
A haunting call that never frees.
Veils of night, shrouded in dread,
What lies ahead? A thread unthreaded.

Eyes that search for light's embrace,
Facing fears, a ghostly race.
Time stands still, yet moves so fast,
A fleeting shadow from the past.

Veins of darkness, heartbeat slow,
The lurking pain, it starts to grow.
A silent plea for dawn's first light,
Hope lingers just out of sight.

As the tide begins to shift,
A moment's pause, a precious gift.
From depths unknown, a spark may rise,
And break the spell with morning skies.

Gazes Crossed

Two souls meet in the crowded room,
A fleeting glance, the air a-bloom.
Hearts collide in the silent space,
Time stands still in the soft embrace.

Eyes like stars, a universe shared,
In that moment, two hearts bared.
Words unspoken paint the night,
Promises held in the soft light.

Each heartbeat echoes, a gentle chime,
Lost in the depth of endless time.
A spark ignites, igniting the flame,
Two strangers never quite the same.

Yet shadows linger, fears take flight,
What if the dawn steals the night?
Gazes crossed, a moment's chance,
An unbroken spell, a timeless dance.

As dawn approaches, they must decide,
To take a leap, to toss aside.
With every step, they face the cost,
In every gain, what's truly lost?

The Anatomy of Thought

Thoughts wander like a restless stream,
Chasing echoes, lost in a dream.
Fragments scatter, like autumn leaves,
Searching for meaning as the mind weaves.

Patterns emerge in the chaos found,
Silent whispers weaving around.
In the silence, ideas collide,
Creating worlds that often hide.

Questions linger, beg for delight,
Clarity blurs in the fading light.
Dancing shadows paint the walls,
Drifting away as the silence calls.

The heart navigates through a maze,
Each twist revealing intricate ways.
In the depths where visions collide,
The essence of self does not abide.

Yet in stillness, a voice may rise,
Carving paths through the clouded skies.
In the chase, we find our worth,
The anatomy of thought births mirth.

Ruminations in the Glass

Gazing into reflections, what do I see?
Fragments lost, yet still they plead.
Moments caught in a fleeting gaze,
Each reflection tells a tale of praise.

Ripples dance within the frame,
Shadows flicker, never the same.
Every face tells a silent plea,
A story sewn in the tapestry.

Battles fought behind the eyes,
Layered truths and sweetened lies.
In the glass, we confront our fears,
And laugh through sorrow, count our tears.

Yet hope glimmers in cracks unseen,
In the stillness, a vivid dream.
To ponder life and all it brings,
In every rift, the heart still sings.

Through the glass, a world to hold,
Stories waiting, yet untold.
Reflections fade but wisdom grows,
In ruminations, our essence flows.

Illusions and Illuminations

In shadows deep, we find our dreams,
A flicker bright, or so it seems.
Reflections twist, the mind will play,
A dance of light that leads astray.

The truth is veiled in colors bold,
While whispers soft, the heart enfold.
Yet in the dark, a spark will glow,
Illuminating paths we know.

What we perceive, a fragile beam,
Like fragile glass, or flowing stream.
Illusions form, yet light reveals,
The hidden wounds, the heart that heals.

We chase the rays, elusive fate,
While shadows linger, contemplate.
In every choice, a lesson learned,
A candle bright, forever burned.

The night shall fade, the dawn shall break,
With every step, our paths awake.
Embrace the light, dispel the mist,
A journey long, we can't resist.

The Dance of Light and Dark

A waltz beneath the silver moon,
Where night and day will meet in tune.
The shadows stretch, the colors blend,
As time itself begins to bend.

In every flicker, tales unfold,
Of dreams that whisper, secrets told.
The sun dips low, the stars ignite,
A tapestry of dark and light.

The flickering flame, the distant star,
Guide lost souls, no matter how far.
In darkness deep, there blooms a spark,
A silent song, a hopeful arc.

The dance continues, never ends,
With every step, new pathways bends.
To find the grace in shadowed plight,
In every tear, there blooms the light.

Embrace the night, don't fear the fall,
For in each shadow, we stand tall.
The balance found, the heart sets free,
In this grand dance of harmony.

Crystal Clear Confessions

In silence deep, the truth will shine,
Like crystal clear, it intertwines.
A fragile heart, a whispered lie,
Yet in the light, we cannot hide.

These thoughts, they swirl, like autumn leaves,
In every sigh, the heart believes.
To share the weight, to bare our soul,
In honesty, we find our goal.

Each word a gem, a silent plea,
To cast away, what's haunting me.
With every glance, the truth unveiled,
An inner strength, once thought curtailed.

Reflections show what's deep inside,
The fears we face, the tears we've cried.
To lift the veil, let darkness flee,
In crystal confessions, we are free.

So take my hand, embrace the light,
Through every storm, we'll rise and fight.
In truths we share, our hearts align,
In crystal clear, our souls entwine.

The Portraits We Hide

Behind the smile, a sorrow set,
In every glance, a tale forget.
The portraits framed, both bright and dim,
Show layers deep, that hide within.

We wear our masks, to shield the pain,
A canvas stained, yet pure as rain.
In every brush, a stroke of fear,
Yet colors bright, forever near.

With every stroke, emotions blend,
A story whispered, curves that bend.
The beauty finds a way to weep,
In colors rich, the secrets keep.

As shadows dance, the light will play,
The art reveals what words can't say.
In every line, a life composed,
In silent truths, the heart exposed.

We paint our dreams with shades of grace,
Each portrait shows a clear embrace.
So let us stand, both strong and proud,
In every hue, we shout aloud.

Delicate Echoes of the Heart

Whispers dance in twilight's grace,
Softened breath in a sacred space.
Each heartbeat sings a gentle song,
In shadows where the dreamers throng.

Tender moments weave like thread,
In tapestry of the things unsaid.
Fleeting glances, a shy embrace,
Time suspends in love's sweet chase.

The heart knows secrets it won't share,
Beyond the surface, feelings rare.
In silent beauty, echoes bloom,
Lingering softly, chasing gloom.

Through fragile paths, we wander still,
Each pulse a testament of will.
Delicate echoes softly chart,
The boundless journey of the heart.

Untold Stories in Glass

Fragments shimmer in faded light,
Whispers trapped in shadows' flight.
Each shard reflects a tale untold,
Memories wrapped in hues of gold.

Moments captured, frozen tight,
In panes of dream, a wondrous sight.
Voices linger within the panes,
Echoing softly, joy and pains.

The morning sun reveals the past,
In every crack, stories amassed.
Glimmers of hope, despair entwined,
In glassy realms, the heart aligned.

We search for meaning in every hue,
In shattered beauty, visions renew.
Untold stories in silence glide,
Reflections of worlds where we abide.

Navigating Through Inward Channels

Inward journeys, a quiet sea,
Where thoughts drift like leaves from a tree.
Currents flow beneath the skin,
Waves of longing draw us in.

Through channels deep, we carve our way,
Finding light in shades of gray.
Echoes resonate, soft and clear,
As we sift through what we hold dear.

The heart maps paths of hidden streams,
Navigating through fragile dreams.
With every turn, we seek to find,
The truth that tugs at heart and mind.

In silence, wisdom starts to bloom,
A tender refuge from the gloom.
Navigating through waters vast,
To embrace the shadows of our past.

Shattered Echoes

When silence falls like shattered glass,
Echoes linger, memories pass.
Fragments whisper in twilight's breath,
A haunting dance with life and death.

Each shard reflects a fleeting time,
In chaos, beauty starts to climb.
Voices trapped in crystal seams,
A symphony of broken dreams.

Through cracks of sunlight, shadows creep,
A tapestry of thoughts we keep.
In every splinter, stories birth,
Capturing the essence of worth.

Shattered echoes, the soul's refrain,
In pain and joy, we learn to gain.
Life's fragile beauty, hard yet true,
In shattered moments, we break through.

The Interlude of Self

In whispers soft, I find my place,
A silent space, a gentle pace.
Thoughts drift like leaves in autumn's breeze,
In this sweet pause, my heart finds ease.

The mirror shows a fleeting glance,
A soul that dances, takes a chance.
Through shadows deep and light's embrace,
I journey on, this sacred space.

In echoes past, the lessons learned,
Through joy and pain, my spirit turned.
Within my core, a flicker glows,
In quietude, my essence flows.

A tapestry of dreams and fears,
Woven with love, and sometimes tears.
This interlude, a soft refrain,
In solitude, I break the chain.

With every breath, I write my song,
A melody where I belong.
In interludes, I find the key,
To open up and set me free.

Fleeting Moments

The clock ticks on, a whisper lost,
In fleeting moments, we pay the cost.
A smile exchanged, a fleeting glance,
These tiny sparks ignite romance.

The sunset paints with colors bright,
A canvas kissed by fading light.
We hold our breath for just a while,
In fleeting moments, time's sweet style.

The laughter shared, the tears we find,
Each fleeting second, intertwined.
Like grains of sand that slip away,
We savor now, come what may.

A breath, a pause, a shifting scene,
In these brief spells, we chase the dream.
For life's a dance, a swirling tune,
In fleeting moments, we find our boon.

So cherish each, both big and small,
For fleeting moments connect us all.
In memories, they softly blend,
These golden threads that never end.

Lasting Impressions

A touch, a glance, a word well said,
In lasting impressions, love is bred.
The laughter shared, the secrets told,
In tiny bonds, our hearts unfold.

Upon the page of time we write,
With every stroke, we breathe life bright.
In whispered tales of days long past,
These lasting memories hold us fast.

Through storms we've faced and skies of gray,
In every moment, we find a way.
A hand to hold, a heart that hears,
In lasting impressions, we conquer fears.

The journeys carved in paths we've walked,
The dreams we've shared, the love we've talked.
These echoes linger, softly pressed,
In lasting impressions, we are blessed.

So let these moments stay with you,
A gift of life in shades of hue.
For in our hearts, they find a home,
In lasting impressions, we are never alone.

Reflections in Moonlight

The silver glow on silent streams,
Reflects our hopes and woven dreams.
Beneath the stars, the night unfolds,
In moonlit whispers, secrets told.

The gentle breeze caresses skin,
As shadows dance where love begins.
In quiet moments, time stands still,
A perfect frame for hearts to fill.

The moonlight bathes the world in peace,
In tender glow, our worries cease.
With every pulse, the night ignites,
Reflections shimmering, soft delights.

In silver beams, we find our way,
Each whispered wish a bright bouquet.
In moonlit nights, our spirits soar,
Reflections of what we adore.

Let every phase remind our hearts,
In twilight's glow, new hope imparts.
For in the dark, we see the light,
Reflections in the moon's soft flight.

Threads of Continuity

In every moment, threads we weave,
A tapestry of love to believe.
Through laughter, tears, and every sway,
These threads of life guide our way.

Connected hearts, both near and far,
In every story, a guiding star.
Through all the storms, we stand as one,
In threads of continuity, we've begun.

With each encounter, roads converge,
In shared experiences, passions surge.
For in the weave, we find our song,
A timeless echo, deep and strong.

In bonds of friendship, love's embrace,
Through every trial, we find our place.
In every thread, a life we mold,
A legacy of warmth to hold.

So cherish well the ties we share,
For every thread shows that we care.
Together onward, hand in hand,
In threads of continuity, we stand.

Refracted Dreams

In twilight's soft embrace, we soar,
Colors blend, forevermore.
Whispers float on liquid air,
Hopes transcend, beyond all care.

Mirrored visions dance and sway,
Guiding hearts along the way.
Fragments scatter in the light,
Drawing paths that feel so right.

Night reveals the hidden hues,
Secrets wrapped in silver clues.
In this realm where wishes gleam,
We awaken from our dream.

The canvas stretches, bold and wide,
Encouraging the soul to glide.
Every heartbeat, every sigh,
Paints the world as we rely.

In refracted beams, we find
Connections forged through heart and mind.
Together woven, never lost,
In this journey, we embrace the cost.

Echoes of Yesterday

Whispers linger in the breeze,
Stories carried through the trees.
Memories dance in the fading light,
Echoes call from the depths of night.

Time's river flows, unbound and free,
Yet shadows cling persistently.
Footsteps trace where we have been,
In every laugh, in every sin.

The past unfolds like petals soft,
In the heart where dreams aloft.
Moments cherished, moments lost,
Carving paths, we bear the cost.

Through faded photographs we gaze,
Retracing steps of youthful days.
Ghostly laughter fills the hall,
In echoes, we remember all.

Yet in the present, life persists,
A blend of joys and misty trysts.
We gather threads to weave anew,
In echoes of the past, we grew.

Tides of Introspection

Gentle waves caress the shore,
Quiet thoughts, a whispered roar.
In the depths, the soul will dive,
Where hopes and fears begin to thrive.

Each ebb and flow, a mirror's face,
Reflecting dreams in this safe space.
Time suspended, moments blend,
In solitude, we find a friend.

The ocean's pulse, a guiding beat,
Leading hearts where fears retreat.
Sheltering thoughts on sandy beds,
Sowing seeds where courage spreads.

The moonlight spills a silver trace,
Illuminating every place.
With each retreat, we learn to breathe,
In the silent waves, we believe.

The tides may shift, yet we remain,
Embracing joy, confronting pain.
In the depths, the light will shine,
Guiding us to intertwine.

The Other Side of Silence

In hushed corners, shadows blend,
Silence speaks, a hidden friend.
Words unspoken hang in air,
Echoes linger, soft and rare.

Between the beats, a truth resides,
In stillness, where the heart confides.
Beneath the noise, a tale unfolds,
An uncharted realm beckons bold.

The whispers weave a fragile thread,
Binding thoughts we fear to shed.
In the quiet, wisdom grows,
Flowing gently, like a rose.

Every pause, a chance to see,
The colors of our empathy.
On the other side, we find,
The spoken depths of heart and mind.

For in this space, we're not alone,
Connection thrives beneath the known.
In silence, we are free to feel,
The other side holds what is real.

The Glass Within

In the depths of glass I gaze,
Shadows dance in silent ways.
A whisper caught in fleeting light,
Mirrors show what hearts ignite.

Each fracture tells a tale untold,
Of dreams embraced, and fears behold.
In crystal shards, the truth appears,
A fragile view, exposed by years.

Reflections shift, a transient form,
In stillness, chaos finds its norm.
The glass within reveals the soul,
A mosaic where the pieces whole.

Layers deep, the moments blend,
Time suspends as illusions mend.
In clarity, the heart can find,
The beauty locked in every mind.

With every glance, a lesson shared,
In the mirror's gaze, we're ensnared.
A journey through the light and shade,
In the glass, our dreams cascaded.

So look inside, and you will see,
The glass within, our history.
Embrace the light, the dark, the grey,
For in each shard, we find our way.

Reflections in Stillness

Upon the water's calm embrace,
I find a moment, time and space.
The world above, a fleeting glance,
Yet down below, reflections dance.

In stillness lies a secret peace,
Where ripples fade and worries cease.
Each droplet tells a tale of dreams,
Unfolding softly, like moonbeams.

The sky above, a canvas wide,
Mirrors what emotions hide.
Each color shifts, a gentle sway,
In quietude, the heart can play.

The silence sings a soothing song,
A melody where we belong.
In nature's hush, the mind unwinds,
Reflections show what life entwines.

With eyes closed tight, I breathe the air,
In solitude, I find a prayer.
Each moment grows, expands the soul,
In stillness, I become whole.

So let the water softly speak,
Reflecting all, both strong and weak.
For in the calm, where stillness stays,
We find ourselves in sacred ways.

The Silent Observer

In shadows cast, I stand apart,
A silent witness, watching hearts.
I see the joy, the pain, the fear,
A tapestry woven, crystal clear.

Through crowded rooms, I drift unseen,
A quiet soul in spaces keen.
Each breath a chapter, every glance,
In hushed tones, life's fleeting dance.

The laughter rings, the tears do flow,
In moments brief, I come to know.
Each story spins, a thread divine,
In silence, truth and fiction twine.

With watchful eyes, I gather all,
The essence of each rise and fall.
In still retreats, the heart's embrace,
I find the pulse of time and space.

The ebb and flow, the light and dark,
In every echo, a poignant mark.
As life unfolds, I stand in grace,
A silent observer, in this place.

For every journey, every turn,
A lesson lives, a truth to learn.
Beyond the noise, I seek what's pure,
In silence, I find a heart's allure.

Fragments of Self

Scattered pieces on the floor,
Fragments of what I was before.
In every shard, a glimpse remains,
A puzzle bound in joy and pains.

Each memory, a tender mark,
Etched in time, a lasting spark.
The laughter, tears, the love, the loss,
All woven tight, despite the cost.

In moments lost, I search to bind,
The echoes of a simpler mind.
A tapestry of hopes and fears,
Frayed edges tell of countless years.

As seasons change, so do I grow,
Embracing all the highs and lows.
In solitude, the self-reflects,
Seeking meaning in its defects.

A mosaic rich, with stories told,
Of passions burned, and dreams enfold.
I gather pieces, stitch by stitch,
Reclaiming fragments, every glitch.

For in this art of self anew,
I find the strength to push on through.
Each fragment sings a different song,
Together, I finally belong.

The Gaze that Bends

In twilight's gleam, the whispers play,
Eyes meet and dance, then drift away.
A fleeting glance, a silent cue,
With every gaze, the heart breaks through.

Reflections linger in the night,
Shadows cast by waning light.
What once was near, now feels so far,
In every look, a silent scar.

The gaze that bends, speaks volumes still,
Unspoken words, a heavy thrill.
Between the breaths, a pause so tense,
A crowded room, yet still so dense.

Secrets shared in glimmers bright,
Two souls entwined in shared delight.
Yet as the dawn begins to rise,
That fleeting spark can fade and die.

So hold the moments, soft and dear,
For in those gazes, love draws near.
And though it bends, it won't erase,
The warmth that lingers in the space.

Shadows of the Soul

In quiet corners, shadows creep,
Darkness holds what we must keep.
Fragments of light break through the night,
Illuminating fears, hidden from sight.

Lost in the maze of silent screams,
Echoes linger, haunting dreams.
Each shadow dances to a tune,
A lullaby sung by the moon.

Whispers carry on the breeze,
Secrets wrapped in stolen pleas.
Between the beats of the heart's refrain,
Lies the truth of joy and pain.

When sunlight fades and night takes hold,
We find our truths in shadows bold.
They shape the world in shades of grey,
A canvas where the spirit lays.

Embrace the darkness, let it be,
For shadows are our memory.
In every curve, where spirits roll,
Lie the sacred shadows of the soul.

Fragments of a Broken Image

Shattered glass on the floor reflects,
A story lost, amidst regrets.
Each piece a glimpse of what once was,
Fleeting moments, without a cause.

Memories rise like morning fog,
Distorted truths, in every smog.
What was whole is now apart,
Each shard holds echoes of the heart.

Searching piecemeal for the whole,
Each fragment whispers to the soul.
Yet in the chaos, beauty blooms,
In brokenness, the light consumes.

Time will mend what life has torn,
Rebuild the dreams we thought were worn.
And in the cracks, the light will gleam,
Making whole the shattered dream.

So cherish each piece, each tiny spark,
For in the dark, we find our mark.
Fragments come together to ignite,
A tapestry woven from the night.

Wading through Transparent Depths

In waters clear, reflections sway,
Thoughts drift like ripples, come what may.
Shadows dance beneath the white,
An endless search in muted light.

With each step, the current pulls,
A gentle guide, the heart it fuels.
Wading through the depths so true,
Unearthing secrets, old and new.

The surface shimmers, beckons still,
To dive deeper, to feel the thrill.
Every wave a story told,
In liquid dreams, our fears unfold.

Patience flows like water's course,
In every drop, resides a force.
Navigating through the vast unknown,
Finding gems in depths unshone.

So wade with grace, let go the dread,
In transparent depths, where dreams are fed.
For in this journey, we embrace,
The reflections that time cannot erase.

www.ingramcontent.com/pod-product-compliance
Ingram Content Group UK Ltd.
Pitfield, Milton Keynes, MK11 3LW, UK
UKHW021301280125
4330UKWH00005B/75

9 781805 609643